PROJECT LOGIC

BE CREATIVE!

IZZI HOWELL

Published in 2025 by Enslow Publishing, LLC
2544 Clinton Street
Buffalo, NY 14224

First published in Great Britain in 2023 by Wayland

Copyright © Hodder & Stoughton Limited, 2023

Editor: Izzi Howell
Consultant: Katherine Muncaster
Series Designer: Rocket Design (East Anglia) Ltd

All rights reserved. No part of this book may be reproduced in any form without permission in writing from the publisher, except by a reviewer.

Manufactured in the United States of America

CPSIA compliance information: Batch #CSENS25: For further information contact Enslow Publishing LLC at 1-800-398-2504.

Please visit our website, www.enslowpublishing.com. For a free color catalog of all our high-quality books, call toll free 1-800-398-2504 or fax 1-877-980-4454.

Cataloging-in-Publication Data

Names: Howell, Izzi.
Title: Be creative! / Izzi Howell.
Description: Buffalo, NY : Enslow Publishing, 2025. | Series: Project logic | Includes glossary.
Identifiers: ISBN 9781978538474 (pbk.) | ISBN 9781978538481 (library bound) |
    ISBN 9781978538498 (ebook)
Subjects: LCSH: Creative ability--Juvenile literature. | Creative ability in children--Juvenile
    literature. | Critical thinking--Juvenile literature. | Logic--Juvenile literature.
Classification: LCC BF408.H68 2025 | DDC 155.4'1335--dc23

Picture acknowledgements:
Shutterstock: BadBrother cover, title page, 4t, 4b, 7t, 7b, 8t, 8b, 11t, 12b, 16, 17t, 17b, 19b, 20b, 21t, 21b, 23t, 23b, 24, 25t, 25b, 26t, 26b, 27, 31t, 31b, 32t, 32b, 33, 35, 37t, 37b, 38t, 41b, 43, 44, 45t, 45b and 46, Rvector and ashimmah 6, AlexTanya 9, Pen-Is Production and wowomnom 11b, Sudowoodo 12t and 45t, LuckyVector and filborg 13, ALX1618 14t, suesse 14b, SpicyTruffel 15, Myvector 17c, art-sonik 18, matsabe 19t, Devita ayu silvianingtyas 20t, Alexander Lysenko 22, 0beron 25c, 28b, 38b and 41t, bsd studio 28t, Tori2 30, Berrypunkid 34t, NesaCera 34b, Polina Tomtosova 39, wowomnom 42.

All design elements from Shutterstock or drawn by designer.

Every effort has been made to clear copyright. Should there be any inadvertent omission, please apply to the publisher for rectification.

CONTENTS

What is creativity? 4
Move the fish 5
Nine dots 9
CREATIVITY IN ACTION: Velcro 14
Odd one out 15
Would you rather? 19
Spelling mistake 23
CREATIVITY IN ACTION: Post-it note 28
Move one glass 29
CREATIVITY IN ACTION: Leonardo da Vinci . . 34
Notebook and pencil 35
Spot the numbers 39
CREATIVITY IN ACTION: Dream-spiration . . . 44
Glossary 46
Challenges 47
Tips 48

WHAT IS CREATIVITY?

Creativity is about being imaginative and finding new ways to solve problems.

Creativity isn't limited to painters, poets, and musicians. It's a skill that is useful in every area of life. For example, a doctor has to think creatively to find different ways to treat a patient if a certain medicine isn't working. Anyone who "thinks outside the box" and challenges themself to see things from another perspective is being creative.

Creativity is a key part of critical thinking. You are less likely to get stuck while trying to solve a problem if you keep an open mind, as you will be willing to try different approaches or even consider "impossible" solutions that might just turn out to be correct.

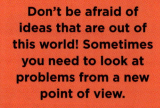

Don't be afraid of ideas that are out of this world! Sometimes you need to look at problems from a new point of view.

Some people are naturally more creative than others, but it is a skill that anyone can work on and improve. It's like a muscle — the more you use it, the stronger it will grow! Doing puzzles that require you to think logically and laterally, such as the ones in this book, will help to boost your creativity.

HOW TO USE THIS BOOK!

Try to solve each puzzle on your own before turning the page and reading the rest of the chapter. Ask an adult for permission before you do any hands-on experiments.

If you need a bit of extra help, check out the

BREAK IT DOWN

section on the page after the puzzle for clues and tips.

Then, check your answer in the **SOLUTION** section.

However, this book isn't just about puzzles. It's about changing the way you think to approach problems in a more logical and creative way. Thinking creatively will help you deal with any challenges that life throws your way!

PUZZLE ONE: MOVE THE FISH

A boy has made a fish out of eight toothpicks. The fish is pointing to the right.

How can you turn the fish around by only moving three toothpicks?

BREAK ↓IT↓ DOWN

Your first instinct may be to try and solve this puzzle in your head. Tricky, right? it's hard to keep track of what you have moved. So why not take the puzzle off the page? Grab a bunch of toothpicks or pencils and recreate the fish.

Now that you have the toothpicks in front of you, it's easier to try out different strategies. Which toothpicks need to move and which ones could stay in the same place? It might help to divide the fish into different parts, such as the body, the head, the fins, and the tail.

Try thinking about how one body part could be changed into another by moving a toothpick. How could the body become a tail or the fins become part of the body?

SOLUTION

As you can only move three toothpicks, the secret to this puzzle is working out how to convert the right-facing fish into a left-facing fish, rather than starting from scratch.

This is where having the toothpicks in front of you helps, since it's really handy to be able to fiddle around and try different approaches.

To make the fish flip over, parts of its tail and fins need to turn into its body and head. The three other toothpicks can then be moved around to fill in the missing pieces.

Move toothpicks 1, 5, and 7 to the new 1a, 5a, and 7a positions.

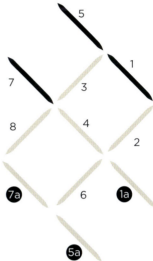

REAL W🌐RLD LOGIC

Whether you are trying to solve a puzzle or learn something new, it's important to be flexible and open-minded. Not every approach works for every situation, and sometimes changing the way you do things can produce better results.

Just like a star-shaped piece and a square hole, some approaches don't match certain tasks!

SAME OLD PROBLEM

As the famous saying goes, "Insanity is doing the same thing over and over again and expecting different results." It's easy to get comfortable with always doing things the same way, but if that approach isn't working, you won't ever make progress!

If you feel frustrated because something isn't working, try doing it a different way!

Try something new

Next time you are struggling to solve a problem, for example one of the challenges in this book, get creative and try approaching it from a different angle. Here are some different methods you could try:

- Make a mind map of the ideas you've had so far
- Draw the puzzle in pictures
- Bounce ideas off other people about the puzzle
- Find objects to represent different parts of the puzzle

"If this one goes here ... maybe that one stays there?"

Explaining your ideas to someone else is a great way of getting them sorted out in your head!

LOGIC TIPS

Different approaches work better for different types of puzzles, so it's important to try lots of things and keep an open mind. Even if an approach worked well when you tried it before, that doesn't mean it's the best fit for your current problem. Likewise, if something didn't work on a previous puzzle, that doesn't mean it won't work for a different type of problem.

Keep going and keep experimenting! You'll get there in the end.

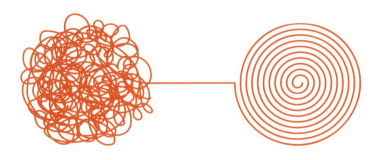

Sometimes you need to try several different approaches to untangle your thoughts and find the right solution!

NINE DOTS

PUZZLE TWO

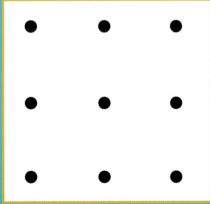

Copy these dots onto a piece of paper. Now try to connect all nine of the dots by drawing four straight lines without lifting your pen off the page or retracing the same line twice.

BREAK ↓IT↓ DOWN

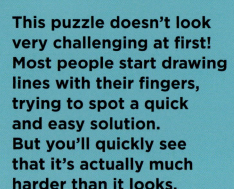

This puzzle doesn't look very challenging at first! Most people start drawing lines with their fingers, trying to spot a quick and easy solution. But you'll quickly see that it's actually much harder than it looks.

What are some possible approaches?

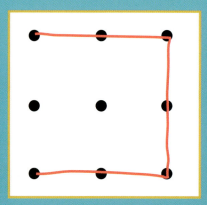

Your first instinct might be to try something obvious, like a square. But what about that dot in the middle?

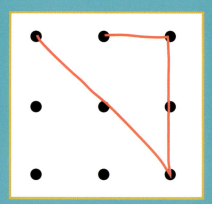

It's a good idea to try other methods, like diagonal lines. But can you find a solution that works?

If you could use five lines, that would be the obvious solution. Some people might get to the stage of using five lines and give up, thinking that that was good enough. But challenge yourself to keep trying, as there is actually a creative solution to this puzzle that connects all nine dots with just four lines.

SOLUTION

The solution to this puzzle requires you to think outside the box … or rather, outside of the grid!

Most people will limit themselves to drawing the lines along the grid of dots, since this is what they think is expected of them. However, if you move the lines off the grid, the solution is simple!

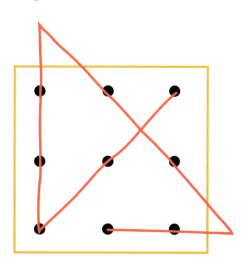

REAL WORLD LOGIC

There are many times in our lives where we create imaginary limits for ourselves. We silence our creativity and force ourselves to follow rules that don't actually exist because of ideas that we have about what we "should" be doing. These rules hold us back in many ways.

DO RULES RULE?

So should we say no to all rules? Well, no, it's not as simple as that! Many rules, such as wearing a seatbelt or waiting for a green light to cross the road, are in place to keep us safe.

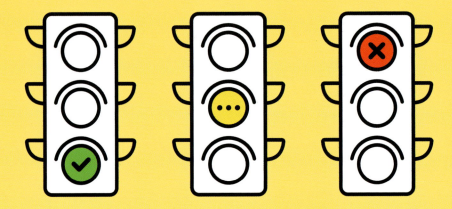

Rule it out

However, some "rules" are officially nonsense! Some people feel like they should never cry in public or that they shouldn't ask for help. These "rules" are unhelpful. And they aren't even rules at all, just things that a few people (incorrectly) believe to be true. Following these kinds of rules can make us feel bad and can stop us from achieving our full potential.

There's nothing wrong with crying. It's a normal, healthy way to express your feelings!

LOGIC TIPS

So how does this connect to puzzles and creativity? If you limit yourself to sticking to the "rules" of how to solve a puzzle, you might not find a creative solution to the problem. Likewise, if you don't let yourself ask for help, you won't be able to learn or make progress.

So why stop here? Get creative and break some more "rules"! Who says that cake has to be sweet? Who says that you have to start a book at the beginning? Who says that you have to paint with a paintbrush? Maybe you'll create a masterpiece!

Cheese, carrot, and cod cake might just be the next big thing!

CREATIVITY IN ACTION: VELCRO

It may seem hard to believe, but a walk in the woods inspired the Velcro found on your bag, shoes, and clothing!

In 1941, Swiss engineer George de Mestral (1907–1990) was walking his dog through the woods when he noticed that his trousers and his dog were covered in spiky seedpods. The seedpods clung tightly to the fabric and fur but could also be easily pulled off.

Ding! A light bulb turned on in de Mestral's head, and he started thinking about how he could use a spiky surface, just like that of the seedpods, to stick other things together.

De Mestral spent the next eight years working on the design for his fastenings. He didn't give up because he believed in himself and his idea. His final product, known as Velcro, used two strips, one covered in tiny hooks and one covered in tiny loops. The two strips firmly stuck together but could also be easily ripped apart.

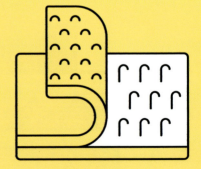

Since then, Velcro has been used as a fastening for many things, from medical equipment and toys to stopping astronauts' pens from floating away in space. And it's all thanks to a walk in the woods! So next time you feel stuck for inspiration, why not change your surroundings and look for creativity elsewhere. You might just get your own light-bulb moment!

Inspiration can sometimes strike in the most unlikely places!

 **ODD ONE OUT**

Choose the odd one out:

Earth	Mars	Saturn	Neptune	Pluto

BREAK ↓IT↓ DOWN

Science fans may think they've found the answer right away. Pluto is the odd one out, since it's the only dwarf planet! But hang on a minute ... is that the only possible answer?

The answer could also be Saturn, since it's the only gas giant, or Earth, since it's the only planet with life on it! Or even that Earth is the odd one out because it's the only one to start with a vowel.

Maybe the solution isn't so simple after all ...

SOLUTION

The solution is actually very simple ... all of those answers were correct! There are multiple correct solutions to this puzzle. It just depends on your perspective. Test your friends and family with this puzzle and see what they come up with. How many different correct answers can you find?

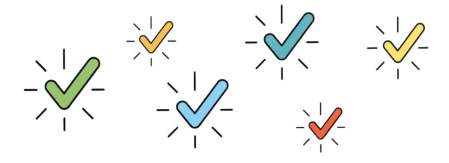

REAL W🌐RLD LOGIC

How do you feel now that you know that there is more than one correct answer? Do you still feel like your first answer is the real solution, even though the others are just as valid? It's quite hard to let go of an idea and make space for other points of view. But questioning yourself and seeing things from other people's perspectives is a key part of thinking critically and creatively.

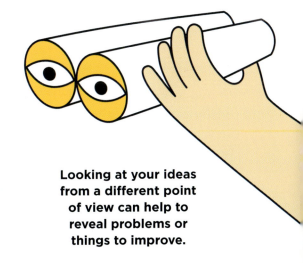

Looking at your ideas from a different point of view can help to reveal problems or things to improve.

A TO B TO C

Our normal way of thinking something through could be drawn as a straight line.

You ask a question, find evidence in the middle, and then stop when you have an answer. This is a great start, but it can mean that you miss out on other ideas or fail to see mistakes in your own work.

Thinking critically needs to look more like a circle. Instead of finishing the line when you've found one answer, why not loop back to the beginning? Can you find another possible answer? Are there any problems with the evidence that you've found? You may end up with lots of circles, and that's absolutely fine! Working in this way helps you to think outside the box and gain insight into other people's points of view.

LOGIC TIPS

Try thinking in a circle next time you approach a problem. Imagine you are a fashion designer who has to design a winter wardrobe. Thick woolly clothes would be warm but itchy, so don't stop there — circle back, check your choices, and get creative! What about layers of thinner fabrics to trap the heat? Or maybe padding like a puffer jacket? All these options will keep you warm, but one may be comfier for you than another. And of course, you probably prefer the look of one style too!

In the real world, it's usually worth looking for different solutions so that you can find the one that suits the task best. With puzzles, most will only have one solution, but reflecting in this way may help you spot a mistake.

 ## WOULD YOU RATHER?

Would you rather have spaghetti hair or cry chocolate tears?

BREAK ↓IT↓ DOWN

Choosing between spaghetti hair or chocolate tears is tough. Chocolate tears sound pretty great – a tasty treat every time you felt sad! But then again, crying chocolate would be incredibly sticky and would probably stain all of your clothes. What a big mess!

So then maybe spaghetti hair? You'd look pretty silly and you'd get lots of questions walking down the street. But it wouldn't be hard to hide under a hat if you didn't want to show it off!

Shhh, no one will ever know!

SOLUTION

Unsurprisingly, this puzzle doesn't have one simple solution. It depends on your opinion. Some people will be totally convinced that spaghetti hair is superior, while others will happily take the chocolate tears.

However, simply stating your point of view isn't quite enough — you need to make a logical, strong argument to back up your opinion.

> Mmm, delicious chocolate tears!

> Chocolate tears would dry hard and lumpy on your face!

> I'd love cool spaghetti hair!

> Spaghetti hair would be impossible to comb.

REAL WORLD LOGIC

Many everyday decisions don't have an obvious answer, such as choosing what to watch on TV or what to eat for a snack. Yet we all have strong opinions about what to watch or eat!

Different people's opinions all have their own strengths and weaknesses. However, there are ways to make your argument stronger.

21

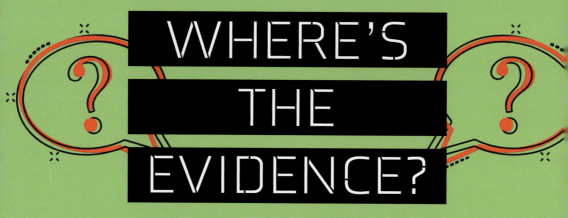

WHERE'S THE EVIDENCE?

It's all very well to say, "I'd rather cry chocolate tears than have spaghetti hair," but you're missing a very important part: *why?* When making an argument, you need to explain why you think this way and use evidence to support your ideas.

COUNTER-ATTACK

It's also a good idea to consider other points of view. This is where creativity comes in, since it can sometimes be hard to see things from the other side.

Then, turn the opposing arguments around and point out their weaknesses. For example, "Spaghetti hair would be less messy than chocolate tears, but it wouldn't taste as good."

LOGIC TIPS

When faced with a situation or a puzzle that doesn't have a clear solution, focus on strengthening your argument. For example, if you're trying to decide what to eat for lunch at home, there are lots of different options that could be good solutions, so it's your job to convince everyone why your idea is the best. Give examples and explain why you think this way (or why you don't). It might be that you already have the ingredients, or that you want to try something new, or that you don't want the other option because you had something similar yesterday!

However, winning an argument isn't really the point of thinking logically. The focus should be on finding the best solution that makes the most sense. And if you explain yourself clearly enough, you may just find that solution!

Warming, healthy and delicious: three reasons we should have soup for lunch!

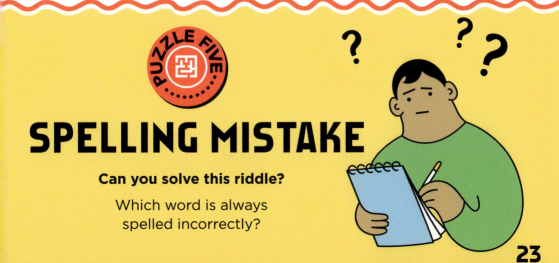

PUZZLE FIVE

SPELLING MISTAKE

Can you solve this riddle?

Which word is always spelled incorrectly?

BREAK ↓IT↓ DOWN

Unlike the previous puzzle, this riddle has only one solution, but it's a tricky one to find! You may feel irritated that you can't figure it out within the first minute or so, which is totally normal. Keep going! You'll never solve it if you give up immediately.

Now is the time to take risks. Brainstorm lots of possible answers to the riddle. It doesn't matter if none of your answers are correct. You're warming up your brain to solve the puzzle, and that's the most important thing.

SOLUTION

Are you ready for the answer? The clue is actually in the question – the word that is always spelled incorrectly is ... incorrectly!

These kinds of "trick questions" can be quite frustrating, since we expect them to work literally. We presume that the answer will be a word that is spelled wrong by most people, but that presumption is just what is holding us back from finding the correct answer.

REAL WORLD LOGIC

Thinking laterally (in a creative way, rather than the normal way) is the key to solving trick questions like this. Our first instincts are often wrong, since they are based on presumptions. Instead, we need to push ourselves to take risks and approach the puzzle in different ways. This may involve coming up with a lot of wrong answers first!

NO WRONG ANSWERS

It may help to hold a "no wrong answers" brainstorming session. It may sound silly, but calling it that might help you to embrace your more out-there thoughts, which might actually be worthy of consideration!

Embrace the impossible

If you are stuck on a problem, why not take a risk on an unlikely idea and dedicate some time to thinking it through? Even if the idea would never work, thinking about something different and unusual might help you to make new connections or find the spark of inspiration you need to work out the answer.

LOGIC TIPS

Our instincts and presumptions are often obstacles to working logically. We get stuck on what we think the answer should be, which makes it hard to find the path to the correct solution.

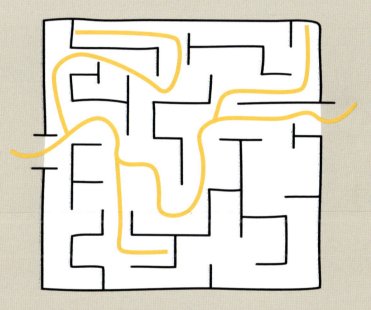

Accepting and considering any ideas, even ridiculous ones, is a brilliant way of pushing past these obstacles. Take a look at the egg drop challenge on page 47 and allow yourself to come up with some silly solutions. What if the egg could fly? What if the shell was made from the hardest material in the world? Now think about how you could make these impossible ideas work in real life.

CREATIVITY IN ACTION: POST-IT NOTE

The story of the Post-it note is a great example of why you should keep going, even if at first you don't succeed!

In 1968, American chemist Dr. Spencer Silver (1941–2021) was trying to invent super-strong glue, but his experiments resulted in an incredibly weak adhesive. Instead of giving up, Dr. Silver got creative and focused on the unique properties of his new invention. His glue could be peeled away and stuck back on again multiple times, unlike stronger glue.

Dr. Silver was convinced that his invention could be useful ... he just didn't know what for! He spent the next five years working on it, but he couldn't come up with a problem that needed his solution.

Inspiration struck in 1974, when a colleague of Dr. Silver's kept losing his bookmark from his choir book. He tried adding Dr. Silver's glue to the bookmark and found that it stayed perfectly in place but could also be repositioned easily.

The two men worked together to develop their discoveries into a new product — the Post-it note! Dr. Silver never gave up on his invention, even though he failed at first. He accepted the challenge to find a use for his new adhesive, and thanks to his creativity and resilience, he came up with a global hit!

Creativity can turn a failure into a fortune!

PUZZLE SIX: MOVE ONE GLASS

Move one glass so that the glasses now look like this:

BREAK ↓ IT ↓ DOWN

If you are able to, taking this puzzle off the page and using real glasses or mugs can help. Give it a try and see if you can solve it yourself!

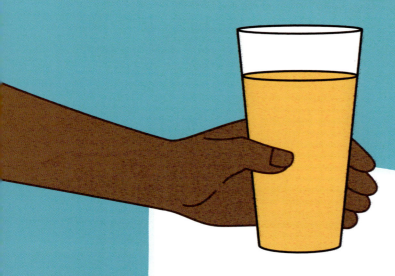

Ready for a clue? As with many problems in this book, it's important to think outside the box. Thinking creatively about the word "move" is a key part of solving this puzzle.

SOLUTION

To solve this puzzle, pick up the second glass from the left and pour its contents into the second glass from the right. Then return the empty glass to its original position. This creates an alternating pattern of empty and full glasses.

REAL WORLD LOGIC

Many people interpret the instructions in this puzzle to mean that they can only move one glass across the table. But movement can be in any direction — up, down, left, right, and even over! There's no reason pouring can't be included.

NO LIMITS

Just as we saw earlier in the Nine Dots puzzle (see pages 9–13), we often create limits for ourselves that can hold us back. This can stop us from reaching the full potential of our creativity. If you get stuck, try rethinking what the question is asking you to do. Could it be reinterpreted in any other way?

Yes limits?

Limits aren't always the enemy of creativity, though. Too much freedom can be overwhelming — how to choose from so many options? Choosing one or two restrictions can push you out of your normal ways of working and force you to look at the problem in a new way. Here are some ideas to try:

- Write a poem without the letter "m"
- Paint a picture with only one color of paint
- Wrap a present without using any tape or string
- Dance with only your face

Getting inside the box can help you think outside it!

LOGIC TIPS

Limits and restrictions can be tricky. They can stop you from thinking logically but can also massively boost your creative thinking power if handled in the right way.

The key is to be in charge. Use limits deliberately to boost your logic and creativity skills, rather than letting them work against you without realizing it!

CREATIVITY IN ACTION: LEONARDO DA VINCI

Leonardo da Vinci (1452–1519) may have lived over 500 years ago, but his imaginative ideas were incredibly forward-thinking!

There wasn't much that Leonardo da Vinci couldn't do — painting, drawing, engineering, science, inventing … the list goes on!

He is well known for his paintings, such as the *Mona Lisa* and *The Last Supper*, but it's in his engineering sketchbooks where Leonardo's creativity and open mind really shine through.

In the 15th and 16th centuries, machines and technology were nowhere near as advanced as they are today. Leonardo didn't let that hold him back in any way and designed a winged flying machine, a self-propelled car, a revolving bridge, and a helicopter. The technology didn't exist to bring his inventions off the page, but the ideas were there, and that's what mattered.

Pushing past the limits of what seems possible opens up a whole new world of creative ideas. Be courageous and abandon what you are familiar with. You might just come up with a solution that you'd never thought of or the next big thing that no one saw coming. Once you have the idea, you can figure out the details later!

LOGIC LESSON

Think and dream big. The rest can follow.

PUZZLE SEVEN: NOTEBOOK AND PENCIL

A notebook and a pencil together cost $1.10. The notebook costs $1 more than the pencil. How much is the pencil?

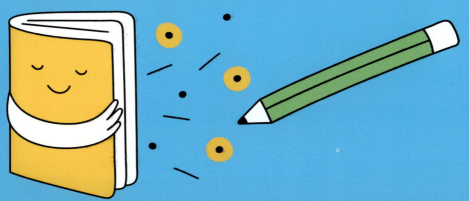

BREAK ↓IT↓ DOWN

Easy — the pencil is 10 cents! But wait ... do you think you might need to check your math, or are you certain that your answer is correct?

Let's double-check ...

Pencil - 10 cents
Notebook - 10 cents + $1 = $1.10

Total = $1.10 (notebook) + 10 cents (pencil) = $1.20

Hmm. Perhaps quick calculations weren't the best solution after all. Maybe it's worth slowing down and thinking before deciding on an answer.

SOLUTION

As we saw before when checking our calculation, the pencil can't be 10 cents or the total would add up to $1.20 instead of $1.10. The pencil is actually 5 cents, making the notebook $1.05 ($1 more), which together add up to the correct total of $1.10!

REAL W🌐RLD LOGIC

Thinking quickly can be an incredibly useful skill. Using our instincts helps us to save time and stay safe by reacting immediately to dangerous situations. However, our instincts can betray us when we're trying to work logically and creatively. Slowing down and checking our work can help us to avoid making silly mistakes.

Don't watch the clock while working logically! Thinking clearly and creatively takes time.

WRITE IT OUT

There's a reason that your math teacher always asks you to show your work! Writing out your calculations or thought process step by step helps to reveal any issues with your reasoning. And if you have made a mistake, it's easy to retrace your steps and find what needs to be corrected.

Been there, done that!

Keeping notes isn't just for math or science. When you're brainstorming creative ideas, it's helpful to record what you've already tried. This will stop you from wasting time by trying the same ideas again and again. However, don't be afraid to revisit wrong answers. Two incorrect answers might just combine together to make a correct one.

Tried, tried, tried, tried ... ooh! That's a new one!

LOGIC TIPS

Slow down when approaching a problem. Your instincts can be valuable, but don't automatically go with your first answer, since you may have made a slipup without realizing. Take time to circle back and check your work.

Writing down your ideas might sound boring, but it's a really powerful creative tool. The simple act of writing or typing your thoughts often gives you a whole new perspective on why your idea is right or wrong. Looking back through your notes can spark new ideas and things to try.

Take it **slowly** ...

PUZZLE EIGHT: SPOT THE NUMBERS

Can you find the following numbers in the number search puzzle on the next page? They can run horizontally, vertically, or diagonally, forward or backward.

178490	352099	516384	882045
264021	437012	650928	916492
285664	402948	782613	903765

NUMBER SEARCH PUZZLE

9	3	1	7	8	2	3	7	2	4	7	5	0	6	4
8	8	2	1	7	8	2	9	1	7	3	8	5	9	8
8	8	4	9	2	0	4	1	0	1	8	3	1	8	0
2	9	7	5	4	5	1	6	7	2	4	2	2	8	2
0	1	6	3	5	7	2	5	3	3	6	5	6	7	6
4	3	5	2	0	9	9	8	4	0	8	9	4	1	4
5	7	8	8	1	7	3	1	7	5	1	6	3	0	3
7	3	2	5	8	5	6	2	9	0	3	7	6	5	5
2	4	6	6	1	3	5	4	6	9	5	1	0	4	4
9	0	8	6	3	4	9	0	6	7	2	9	8	5	0
7	6	3	4	0	2	6	2	8	0	6	5	4	7	9
5	8	1	3	8	1	1	7	4	1	9	3	3	3	4
4	2	2	7	3	5	2	6	5	0	9	2	8	1	8
8	3	0	9	6	8	2	3	2	4	1	8	4	2	7
2	9	4	6	1	9	0	9	3	2	8	5	5	1	1

178490
264021
285664
352099
437012
402948

516384
650928
782613
882045
916492
903765

BREAK IT DOWN

Spotting details in a big, complicated image like this is tough. Your brain gets distracted by the other numbers, and you often find yourself checking the same places over and over again.

Find the solution to this puzzle on page 42 — no peeking!

Strangely enough, walking away from a puzzle like this is often the secret to solving it! If you're having a hard time finding the numbers, why not try taking a break and coming back to it later. It sounds silly, but sometimes being creative is about testing new strategies … even if they sound ridiculous! You'll be surprised how quickly you find the rest of the missing numbers.

REAL WORLD LOGIC

Forcing yourself to keep working at a puzzle or creative problem that you are struggling with is often a waste of time. Your brain can't work at its best when it is overloaded and overwhelmed. So taking a break can be the best use of your time.

It's hard to think logically when your energy bar is low! Recharge your brain by taking a break.

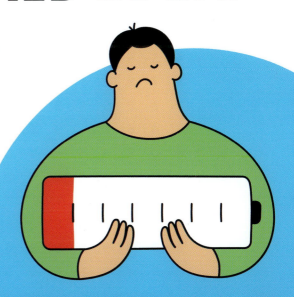

BACKGROUND BRAIN

Have you ever tried to remember something, given up, and then suddenly remembered it hours or even days later? Amazing, right? This happens because the brain keeps on working on problems in the background even once you've stopped actively thinking about them.

SOLUTION

LOGIC TIPS

If you can't figure something out, put your brain to work while you take a well-deserved rest! Go outside, play a game, listen to music, or even take a nap! Try to forget the problem, and let your brain think it over while you're having fun.

You may suddenly realize the solution when you least expect it. Even if you don't get a flash of inspiration, the problem should seem easier when you go back to it with a fresh mind.

CREATIVITY IN ACTION: DREAM-SPIRATION

You've probably had funny dreams, scary dreams, and seriously strange dreams, but have you ever had a dream that solved a problem?

Over the years, various scientists and great thinkers have reported dreaming the answer to questions they had been struggling with while awake.

At the end of the 19th century, Russian chemist Dmitri Mendeleev (1834–1907) was searching for a way to organize Earth's known elements into some sort of system. He tried and tried but couldn't find a solution that made sense.

One night, he dreamt that he saw the elements falling into place in a table. When he woke up, he realized that the elements in the table he had dreamt were arranged by their relative atomic mass. This system worked perfectly, and the periodic table as we know it today was born!

Mendeleev wasn't the only one with helpful dreams. When the German chemist Friedrich Kekulé (1829–1896) was trying to work out the structure of the substance benzene, he had a dream of a snake biting its own tail. When he woke up, he realized that benzene had a ring-shaped structure, just like the snake in his dream!

And it's not just science. The author Mary Shelley (1797–1851) based her novel *Frankenstein* on an idea that came to her in a dream!

LOGIC LESSON

Never underestimate the power of rest and relaxation!

GLOSSARY

adhesive – a sticky substance used for joining things together

approach – a way of doing or thinking about something

argument – a reason or reasons you agree or disagree with something

back up – to support

brainstorm – to suggest lots of possible ideas very quickly

evidence – one or more reasons you believe something is true or untrue

instinct – a natural way of acting without thinking

interpret – to decide what something means

lateral thinking – thinking about something in a creative way, rather than the expected way

logic – a way of thinking about something very carefully to understand it

mind map – a diagram used to visually organize information

obstacle – something that blocks you from moving forward or makes movement more difficult

perspective – a particular way of considering something

presumption – believing that something is true without having any proof

reasoning – thinking about something in order to make a decision

resilience – being happy and willing to try again after something difficult has happened

strategy – a way of doing something

valid – able to be accepted

CHALLENGES

Now that you have lots of tips for thinking creatively, consider how you'd approach some of these challenges and give them a try! If you need a hint, check out the tips on page 48.

1 Using everyday items, design a way to protect an egg from breaking when dropped from a height.

2 Make an outfit from cardboard.

3 Draw 30 identical circles on paper. Then, try to turn as many circles as possible into recognizable objects in just three minutes.

4 Build the longest marble run possible. Use materials of your choice.

5 Make as many different objects as possible out of five blocks.

TIPS

1 Adding padding and protection to your egg is important, but slowing down its fall can also be effective.

2 Joining smaller pieces of cardboard together will help you create shapes that fit the body better.

3 "Break the rules" as much as you like! Why not combine two circles to make a pair of glasses? What could you make from three or four circles connected together?

4 Consider different approaches for different materials. You could build a flat marble run using blocks or a vertical marble run by sticking cardboard tubes together using masking tape.

5 Think about what the different blocks can represent. They could be body parts, sections of a building or a machine, or even combined together to make the shape of a country! The only limit is your imagination.